THIS PLANNER BELONGS TO:

Meet the Author
DR. COURTNEY DAVIS
EDUCATOR. AUTHOR. PODCASTER.

GET READY...
GET SET...

Congratulations!

YOU HAVE DECIDED TO BEGIN THE JOURNEY TO LAUNCH YOUR STORYBOOK.

Becoming an author is one of the most exciting, rewarding experiences of your life. As an author of three well-loved children's books and a publishing coach to several authors, I can imagine everything that you're feeling, thinking, and asking yourself about this process.

That's exactly why you are in the right place. When I set out to write and self-publish my first book, I had no clue what I was getting myself into. As an educator, I knew that I wanted to write a book that told a beautiful story and helped children to see themselves differently and learn something along the way. I had a dream of putting my book out into the world, inspiring lots of little readers, and creating lots of smiles.

I did that. But the road was not exactly as easy as I expected it to be. Once I made the decision to really write a book, I realized that there was so much more to putting words on a page. I needed to get really clear about the story I wanted to tell. I needed to create time in my super busy schedule to actually write. I had to find the right professionals to get my book published. (Because dreams take teams!) It took a lot of sweat, tears, and overcoming fears to get my first book done and into the world. But I did it. Then I did it again.

Now I am passionate about helping other authors, like you, to find their way through this process so they can do it too.

If you picked up this planner, you have a story to share. You want that story to teach and delight children. You want your books to build a legacy for you. All of that is possible by self-publishing your children's storybook!

You were born to do this. You just need a little help along the way. I created this planner to provide you with that help. Designed to be the ideal jumpstart to your book publishing journey, these pages will get your creative juices flowing, show you how to plan out your book, and find the right people to help you to bring your dream book to life.

THIS PLANNER WILL:

- 🚀 **Ease your fears** around writing and publishing a children's book on your own.

- 🚀 **Identify** the time and space to write your storybook.

- 🚀 **Help** you to map out the vision for your book.

- 🚀 **Build** your self-publishing Success Squad.

- 🚀 **Create** a budget for your storybook.

- 🚀 **Share** ideas to promote your book.

- 🚀 **Plan** your book launch.

ARE YOU READY? LET'S GET TO WORK!

LET'S TALK ABOUT *you!*

How long have you been a writer?

Who inspired you to become a writer?

Describe your talents that make you an awesome writer.

When you write, do you prefer to type, transcribe, or write your drafts?

When did you decide that you wanted to write a children's storybook?

How long have you dreamed of self-publishing your book?

What's the title of your favorite children's book? Why?

If you could be the best friend of any children's book author, who would you choose?

Do you have a favorite illustrator? Who?

feelings CHECK-IN

When you think about the journey that you are about to begin, how do you feel? *(Circle all emotions that apply.)*

- 😆 Excited
- 😳 Terrified
- ☹️ Anxious
- 😃 Enthusiastic
- 😵 Scared

- 😊 Delighted
- 😍 Inspired
- 🙁 Overwhelmed
- 😠 Determined
- 😉 Adventurous

YOUR AUTHOR'S *checklist*

To become a self-published author, there is a list of things to do in addition to writing the story. You will create the story AND

- ⭐ **Identify** Your Reader
- ⭐ **Design** The Book Cover
- ⭐ **Build** An Audience
- ⭐ **Identify** Other Professionals To Help Get The Book Done
- ⭐ **Develop** A Social Media Campaign
- ⭐ **Post** On Social Media
- ⭐ **Monitor** Your Book Inventory
- ⭐ **Autograph** And Send Books To Your Young Readers At Home, Schools - Across The Country
- ⭐ **Track** The Income And Pay All Bills
- ⭐ **Market** Your Book To An Audience
- ⭐ **Create** And Monitor The Related Merchandise
- ⭐ **Pay** Your Taxes
- ⭐ **Schedule** Appearances At Local Events, Schools, And Festivals
- ⭐ **Coordinate** Zoom Meetings, Panel Discussions, And Mastermind Meetings With Readers And Colleagues To Build Community

Is there anything on this list that you have no idea how to do? Are you worried about doing everything on your own? For now, focus on one thing....

YOUR *why!*

WHY do you want to write this storybook?

WARNING: Do not proceed without writing your response!
The answer to this question will provide the extra oomph to push through all the activities that have nothing to do with the writing and everything to do with self-publishing! When times get tough, your WHY will keep you rooted and able to push through the yucky stuff to ultimately launch your storybook.

the TIME AUDIT

Writing a book is a major time commitment. The amount of time that it will take for you to write your book depends on a number of factors including how you like to create, what you need to get motivated, and how much time you have. But the bottom line is books don't write themselves!

Setting aside dedicated time in your hectic schedule to write is a must. The time to write your book is there. You just have to find it. **Think about how you spend your time.**

Track your time for the next two weeks. Using whatever calendar you like to use, write down the following:

- ⭐ What time you wake up

- ⭐ All your daily activities, including breakfast, lunch, and dinner. *(Don't forget to include the time to take the dog for a walk, drop off or pick up little ones from the babysitter and reading a magazine too!)*

- ⭐ What time you crash at the end of the day

Believe it or not, we all tend to overestimate or underestimate how we spend our time during a day. However, when we track our time, we begin to see trends.

When is your most creative time of day?

Which day/time do you feel most energetic?

What day/time do you feel pooped?

IMPORTANT QUESTION:

When do you have time to work on your storybook? Once you identify the time, mark it on your planner.

What will you do to protect your writing time?

1.

2.

3.

your WRITING ROOM

To write your book, you don't just need time—you need physical space. We all have our special places where we go to create. Let's find yours.

Describe your optimal place to write.

Do you need a desk and sturdy chair?

Are you lounging on an outside deck, park, or beach?

Can you write with a bit of music playing, people chatting in the background or do you need total silence?

What do you like to wear while writing? Is it a sweat top and bottoms, cozy socks, or your fave PJs?

notes:

SAY OUT LOUD IN FRONT OF A MIRROR,

I AM *ready* TO BEGIN MY SELF-PUBLISHING *journey!*

reflection...

DO YOUR homework

You have to start somewhere! Many of us can begin the adventure of writing and publishing our storybooks by stretching out fingers and using a favorite search engine: Google!

One of the most important first steps you can take is Googling "SELF-PUBLISHING CHILDREN'S BOOKS"!! There is a tsunami of blogs, articles, and books to give you enough information to take initial action.

In addition to the information that you'll gather online, there are so many other ways to learn about the self-publishing process. **Here are a few suggestions:**

- ⭐ Reach out to a local publisher and see if they offer free workshops or courses.

- ⭐ Identify and purchase a self-published children's book that you love! Reach out to the author and make an appointment to chat. Share why you are inspired by the book and ask a few questions.

- ⭐ Listen to podcasts like @The Way We Self-Publish.

- ⭐ Attend conferences or workshops about self-publishing.

- ⭐ Attend specialty events at local bookstores.

- ⭐ Go to the local university and reach out to their English department to speak to professors or attend events in the department.

- ⭐ Reach out to an independent bookstore, get a roster of their events, and GO!

- ⭐ Visit your local public library and make friends with the children's librarian (they know so much awesome information).

- ⭐ Join a writing organization that caters to children's books.

- ⭐ Contact the librarian at a local public school.

- ⭐ Join a meet-up or local group that has a focus on writing stories for children and teens.

IMPORTANT

AVOID asking another self-published author for their time without doing YOUR homework first! Many answers to your questions can be found with a little time online.

AVOID saying the following statement: Can you tell me everything you know about self-publishing in about 5 minutes? Can I pick your brain? Instead, come prepared with a list of well-researched questions to show that you've at least done some homework on your own.

notes

TAKE SOME *field trips*

A great writer is a great reader. Before penning your own book, take the opportunity to become familiar with other children's books, particularly books with a similar topic. Visit your local public library and become friends with the children's librarian! They know everything about children's books. Librarians can tell you about award-winning authors, illustrators, standards for books, and strategies to attract the attention of young readers. Make them your bestie!

Local Librarian:	
Phone:	
Email:	
Address:	

Local Librarian:	
Phone:	
Email:	
Address:	

Don't stop with a single visit to the library! Let's take a trip to the local independent bookstore too. There, you may find more self-published children's books, coloring books, and workbooks by your favorite author.

Be prepared to spend some time walking along the aisles and observing the book covers. Which ones jump out at you? Which colors are you attracted to? Which images are located on the front and back of the books? Take note of all these elements to determine what you'd like to see in your own book.

⭐ **Talk** to the bookseller and begin to develop a relationship. They know a lot about books!

⭐ **Ask** about networking opportunities for writers.

⭐ **Inquire** about books that are popular, top-sellers, and related to the topic of your book.

QUESTIONS TO CONSIDER:

Based on the books that you've seen, have you noticed any patterns?

What's the price of books that are similar to yours?

What is the size of the book that you want to create? 8.5 x 11, 5 x 7, or smaller?

notes

the GENRE & AGE GROUP

What genre of book will you create? *(Choose one.)*

⭐ **Fiction** = an imagined story

⭐ **Non-fiction** = facts or real-life experiences

⭐ A lil' bit of both

What type of book will you create? *(Choose one.)*

⭐ **Board Book** *(Newborn to age 3)*

These books are made of paperboard and are ideal for the youngest children.

⭐ **Picture Book** *(Ages 3 - 8)*

These books are full of fun and adventure! They will engage the reader and are filled with pages of vivid illustrations. A lot of adults like these stories too!

⭐ **Early Reader Book** *(Ages 5 - 9)*

These books reflect a middle ground (or a bridge) between picture books and chapter books. The plot is very simple for this group of readers who are learning to read independently.

⭐ **Chapter Book** *(Ages 7 - 10)*

Chapter books reflect their name and usually have short chapters to encourage young readers who are continuing to be independent learners. They can address issues in school and family relationships with simple plot twists.

⭐ Middle Grade (Fiction) Book *(Ages 9 - 12)*

Preteens can be protagonists in these books. Typically, self-reflection is not a theme. There is a focus on relationships with family and friends and their experiences within a smaller, limited community.

⭐ Young Adult Fiction (YA) Book *(Ages 13 and up)*

Protagonists are typically older teenagers. These books are generally longer and focus on the internal conflict, self-reflection, and issues related to adjusting to an adult world. Though these books are written for teens, there are some very mature and adult themes permitted in the novel.

notes

describe YOUR BOOK

What are some words to describe your book? *(Circle all stars that apply.)*

- ⭐ Full Of Jokes
- ⭐ Funny
- ⭐ Historical
- ⭐ A Story That Solves A Problem
- ⭐ Takes Place At An International Location
- ⭐ Adventurous
- ⭐ Political
- ⭐ Mystery
- ⭐ Has Bilingual Text

- ⭐ Highlights A Special Place or Community
- ⭐ Includes Characters From Another Planet
- ⭐ Has A Funky Rhythm
- ⭐ Focuses On Science
- ⭐ Talks About Your Favorite Pet
- ⭐ Takes Place Underwater
- ⭐ Rhymes
- ⭐ Includes Wacky Animals

notes

notes

shape YOUR STORY

What's the name of the main character?

Describe the main character.

What will the main character do in the story?

Does the adventure take place in your backyard or on another planet?

Will your story include dragons that the wear tutus?

Does your story include magical dust that makes all the dogs go to sleep?

Brainstorm a few ideas for your book:

1.

2.

3.

4.

the READER

Describe the reader of your storybook. Who is the target audience for your book? *Be specific.*

Name:	
Hair:	
Gender:	
Age:	
Height:	
Behaviors:	
Clothing:	
Additional information:	

DRAW A PICTURE OF THE READER WHO WILL MOST ENJOY YOUR CHILDREN'S BOOK.

GET SOME *goals*

As writers, we are plagued by to-do lists and deadlines. However, we can use it to our advantage. We need to develop goals to help to dictate our daily actions. You know how much time you have in a day. You know the multiple tasks that need to be completed. Now, let's create the goals to help launch the storybook!

There are two parts to the goal: 1. identify the action you want to take and 2. the timeframe to complete the task. **Write out 3-5 goals to help you get your book done!**

3.

4.

5.

THE SUCCESS *squad*

The Success Squad is the group of professionals that can assist with launching your storybook. They include:

- ⭐ Editor
- ⭐ Graphic Designer
- ⭐ Illustrator
- ⭐ Webmaster
- ⭐ Layout Designer
- ⭐ Photographer
- ⭐ Event Planner
- ⭐ PR Specialist
- ⭐ Social Media Expert
- ⭐ Book Coach/Mentor
- ⭐ Printer
- ⭐ Marketer
- ⭐ Accountant

Stop! You don't have to feel overwhelmed yet! You don't need all these extra squad members now. But many self-published authors attempt to fill every one of these roles themselves in addition to writing the storybook! Big mistake! You need help.

In the beginning, there is only one role that requires your prioritized attention: Writer! Focus on writing the best story possible. You will write, rewrite, write some more, rewrite some more. Next, send your material to the editor. The editor will provide feedback and you will rewrite some more. You may feel like you are on a merry-go-round with the editor. Then TAH-DAH! We have a final manuscript!

notes

FINDING AN EDITOR

There are many ways to find the right editor for your book. You can:

⭐ Request a referral from a fellow writer.
⭐ Search online resources for a seasoned editor.
⭐ Talk to writers in your social media or writing group and discuss their experiences when working with an editor.

QUESTIONS

» What experience do you have with editing children's books?
» What is your rate?
» Please share the process for us to work together.
   (The editor will share their workflow and number of drafts to provide.
» Request referrals from the editor.

Editor's Name:	
Email:	
Social Media:	

Editor's Name:	
Email:	
Social Media:	

Editor's Name:	
Email:	
Social Media:	

PARTNERING WITH THE PERFECT ILLUSTRATOR

Do you know how to create illustrations for a children's book?

Neither did I! If I was the illustrator, my books would be filled with stick figures.

As soon as you have a concept for your story, take the time to research illustrators and their diverse styles. Here are a few ways to find an illustrator:

- ⭐ Look at lots of self-published books and check out the name of the illustrator. Visit their website or social media account.
- ⭐ Visit your local university and reach out to art professors and students.
- ⭐ Create an ad and display it in a bookstore, coffee shop, art supply store, etc.
- ⭐ Request a referral from a writer, colleague, or fellow creative.
- ⭐ Follow social media groups that are tailored to illustrators.

QUESTIONS

- » Do you like their style? Is it appropriate for the reader?
- » When is the artist available?
- » Is there a waiting list for the artist?
- » Name 3-5 illustrators and collect their contact information.

Questions to Ask an Illustrator

- » May I see your portfolio and reach out to any satisfied customers?
- » Do you have experience with creating images for a picture book?
- » Do you have experience with uploading illustrations to Ingram Spark or KDP (name the identified platform)?
- » Do you have a standard rate for a children's book with 28 pages?
- » Is there a different cost for a 2-page image rather than a single page image?
- » What is the timeframe for a project?
- » What is the schedule to pay for the illustrations?

CONTACT INFORMATION FOR POTENTIAL ILLUSTRATORS

Name 3-5 illustrators and collect their contact information.

Illustrator's Name:	
Description of Illustration:	
Email:	
Social Media:	

Illustrator's Name:	
Description of Illustration:	
Email:	
Social Media:	

Illustrator's Name:	
Description of Illustration:	
Email:	
Social Media:	

Illustrator's Name:	
Description of Illustration:	
Email:	
Social Media:	

Illustrator's Name:	
Description of Illustration:	
Email:	
Social Media:	

promoting YOUR BOOK

CREATING A WEBSITE

Currently, it is a general rule that any service or item for sale requires a website. That includes your storybook! Your readers and fans need a way to find YOU and your storybook. How are they supposed to do that? That's right. A website.

Your website is your calling card for readers and their parents to reach out to you to share feedback, their photos with your books, and to order books.

Because you are starting out, just focus on the basic information. **Your website should have the following features or pages:**

- ⭐ Home Page
- ⭐ About Page
- ⭐ Buy My Book Page
- ⭐ Press & Reviews Page
- ⭐ Contact Page

You have visited (or stalked) several authors and their websites by now. Visit their websites and identify features that you would like to adopt on your own website.

QUESTIONS

» Will you make your site engaging for young readers or is it strictly for parents?

» Do you need a head shot right now?

» Are you comfortable writing your own content for the site?

» Can you design the site yourself, or do you need to hire someone?

CHOOSING A DOMAIN NAME

Identify 4-5 possible domain names for your website. (That is your **www.[insert name].com.**)

1. _____

2. _____

3. _____

4. _____

5. _____

Now, research the names to see if they are already reserved. If not, GET IT as soon as possible.

SOCIAL MEDIA

Which social media platforms will you use to reach your target audience? **Choose two options.** *(You can always add more social media accounts later. I just want you to get started!)*

Facebook • Tik Tok • Instagram • Twitter • YouTube • Clubhouse

1. _____   2. _____

BOOK FESTIVALS ARE A MARKETING MACHINE!

Festivals are awesome opportunities to promote your book, meet readers, and increase sales!

QUESTIONS

- Who is the target market that will attend this event?
- How many attendees are you expecting?
- Will you provide a table, chairs and access to electricity?
- What are the times to set up and close down my display?
- Are there height requirements for a display in my area?
- Is there an extra fee if I bring an additional team member?
- How much is the registration fee for the event? What is the payment plan?
- When is the final payment due?
- Is this event specifically highlighting authors of children's books?
- Am I the only author of (name the identified topic)?
- Will volunteers be available to assist in moving items to and from my car?

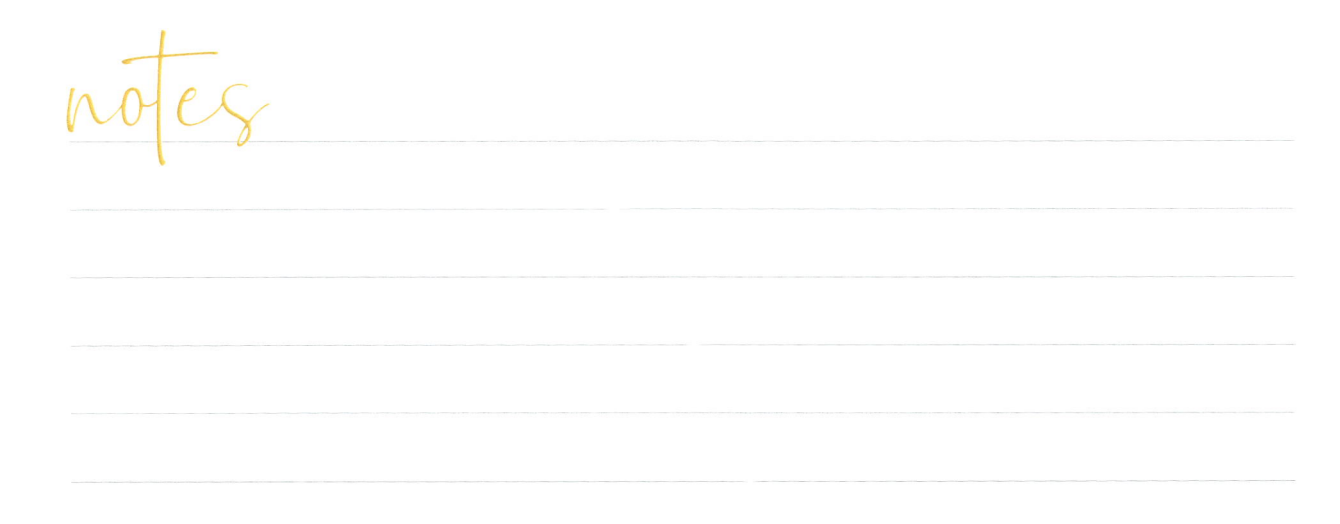

notes

IN – PERSON BOOK FESTIVAL CHECKLIST

⭐ **1 month in advance** – Place the event on your website. Your readers want to know about you and your events!

⭐ **2 weeks in advance** – If you intend to participate in several book festivals, you may want to purchase a cart to easily transfer your items to the specified area.

⭐ **1 week in advance** – Make sure to share your event on all social media platforms. Encourage readers to attend your event and increase the BUZZ and excitement!

⭐ **1 week in advance** – Share the event hashtag on social media.

⭐ **Day before the event** – Review the contract to participate in the book festival. Make sure you understand the regulations related to space, provision of a table and chair, and access to electricity and an audio system.

⭐ **Day before the event** – Pack extra pens, paper, tape, markers and a pair of scissors in a package ready to go.

⭐ **Day before the event** – Choose your table cover for the event.

⭐ **Day of event** – Bring snacks and water.

⭐ **Day of event** – Wear comfortable shoes and clothing.

⭐ **Day of event** – Feel free to create a display highlighting your logo, identified colors, and your book.

⭐ **Day of event** – Bring cell phone and everything you need to sell books and take pictures with readers for promotional purposes.

⭐ **Day of event** – Chat with the coordinator to locate the restroom.

the 6 - LETTER WORD

It's time to chat about the B-word! That's B-U-D-G-E-T! As aspiring writers who want to self-publish books for children and teens, there's no way we can avoid talking about the money to make it happen. Say Ka-ching!!

When it comes to your book, there may be some tasks that you choose to take on yourself to save money (or because you are great at it) and others that you will outsource to a professional on your Success Squad. Either way, when we begin the journey to self-publish, you must create a budget. I promise you will thank me later!

IMPORTANT QUESTIONS:

How much is it going to cost to produce this book?

_____
_____
_____
_____
_____

How much will it cost to work with an editor?

_____
_____
_____
_____
_____
_____

How much will it cost for the illustrations?

_____
_____
_____

Are there any advertisement costs associated with the project?

_____
_____
_____

What are the printing costs associated with the initial 50 copies of the book?

_____
_____
_____

TOTAL ESTIMATED BUDGET:

Once you identify the initial costs to produce your book, check your bank account. If the money is in the bank, that's awesome news! If not, start saving your coins ASAP! It is very easy to waste money, but you can avoid a financial catastrophe because you have a plan.

you CAN DO IT!

JUST A FEW LAST DETAILS...

⭐ Become a member of a writing community or network.

⭐ Tell every friend, family member, and colleague that you have self-published a book. Spread the word!

⭐ Participate in book festivals and podcasts about your journey.

⭐ Create a press release and distribute it to local and regional outlets.

⭐ Join social media groups to share experiences and ask questions.

notes

this month:

MONTH:

YEAR:

SUNDAY	MONDAY	TUESDAY	WEDNESDAY	THURSDAY

FRIDAY	SATURDAY

notes

this week: _____

MON.	
TIME	SCHEDULE

THOUGHTS FOR MY BOOK:

_____
_____
_____
_____
_____
_____
_____

TUE.	
TIME	SCHEDULE

THOUGHTS FOR MY BOOK:

_____
_____
_____
_____
_____
_____
_____

WED.	
TIME	SCHEDULE

THOUGHTS FOR MY BOOK:

_____
_____
_____
_____
_____
_____
_____

THU.

TIME	SCHEDULE

THOUGHTS FOR MY BOOK:

FRI.

TIME	SCHEDULE

THOUGHTS FOR MY BOOK:

SAT.

TIME	SCHEDULE

THOUGHTS FOR MY BOOK:

SUN.

TIME	SCHEDULE

THOUGHTS FOR MY BOOK:

this week: _____

MON.	
TIME	SCHEDULE

TUE.	
TIME	SCHEDULE

WED.	
TIME	SCHEDULE

THOUGHTS FOR MY BOOK:

THOUGHTS FOR MY BOOK:

THOUGHTS FOR MY BOOK:

THU.

TIME	SCHEDULE

THOUGHTS FOR MY BOOK:

FRI.

TIME	SCHEDULE

THOUGHTS FOR MY BOOK:

SAT.

TIME	SCHEDULE

THOUGHTS FOR MY BOOK:

SUN.

TIME	SCHEDULE

THOUGHTS FOR MY BOOK:

this week: _____

MON.	
TIME	SCHEDULE

TUE.	
TIME	SCHEDULE

WED.	
TIME	SCHEDULE

THOUGHTS FOR MY BOOK:

THOUGHTS FOR MY BOOK:

THOUGHTS FOR MY BOOK:

THU.

TIME	SCHEDULE

THOUGHTS FOR MY BOOK:

FRI.

TIME	SCHEDULE

THOUGHTS FOR MY BOOK:

SAT.

TIME	SCHEDULE

THOUGHTS FOR MY BOOK:

SUN.

TIME	SCHEDULE

THOUGHTS FOR MY BOOK:

this week: _____

MON.	
TIME	SCHEDULE

TUE.	
TIME	SCHEDULE

WED.	
TIME	SCHEDULE

THOUGHTS FOR MY BOOK:

THOUGHTS FOR MY BOOK:

THOUGHTS FOR MY BOOK:

THU.

TIME	SCHEDULE

THOUGHTS FOR MY BOOK:

FRI.

TIME	SCHEDULE

THOUGHTS FOR MY BOOK:

SAT.

TIME	SCHEDULE

THOUGHTS FOR MY BOOK:

SUN.

TIME	SCHEDULE

THOUGHTS FOR MY BOOK:

this week: _____

MON.	
TIME	SCHEDULE

TUE.	
TIME	SCHEDULE

WED.	
TIME	SCHEDULE

THOUGHTS FOR MY BOOK:

THOUGHTS FOR MY BOOK:

THOUGHTS FOR MY BOOK:

THU.

TIME	SCHEDULE

THOUGHTS FOR MY BOOK:

FRI.

TIME	SCHEDULE

THOUGHTS FOR MY BOOK:

SAT.

TIME	SCHEDULE

THOUGHTS FOR MY BOOK:

SUN.

TIME	SCHEDULE

THOUGHTS FOR MY BOOK:

END OF MONTH *reflection*

this month:

MONTH: **YEAR:**

SUNDAY	MONDAY	TUESDAY	WEDNESDAY	THURSDAY

FRIDAY	SATURDAY

notes

this week: _____

MON.	
TIME	SCHEDULE

TUE.	
TIME	SCHEDULE

WED.	
TIME	SCHEDULE

THOUGHTS FOR MY BOOK:

THOUGHTS FOR MY BOOK:

THOUGHTS FOR MY BOOK:

THU.

TIME	SCHEDULE

THOUGHTS FOR MY BOOK:

FRI.

TIME	SCHEDULE

THOUGHTS FOR MY BOOK:

SAT.

TIME	SCHEDULE

THOUGHTS FOR MY BOOK:

SUN.

TIME	SCHEDULE

THOUGHTS FOR MY BOOK:

this week: _____

MON.	
TIME	SCHEDULE

THOUGHTS FOR MY BOOK:

_____
_____
_____
_____
_____
_____
_____
_____

TUE.	
TIME	SCHEDULE

THOUGHTS FOR MY BOOK:

_____
_____
_____
_____
_____
_____
_____
_____

WED.	
TIME	SCHEDULE

THOUGHTS FOR MY BOOK:

_____
_____
_____
_____
_____
_____
_____
_____

THU.

TIME	SCHEDULE

THOUGHTS FOR MY BOOK:

FRI.

TIME	SCHEDULE

THOUGHTS FOR MY BOOK:

SAT.

TIME	SCHEDULE

THOUGHTS FOR MY BOOK:

SUN.

TIME	SCHEDULE

THOUGHTS FOR MY BOOK:

this week: _____

MON.	
TIME	SCHEDULE

TUE.	
TIME	SCHEDULE

WED.	
TIME	SCHEDULE

THOUGHTS FOR MY BOOK:

THOUGHTS FOR MY BOOK:

THOUGHTS FOR MY BOOK:

THU.

TIME	SCHEDULE

THOUGHTS FOR MY BOOK:

FRI.

TIME	SCHEDULE

THOUGHTS FOR MY BOOK:

SAT.

TIME	SCHEDULE

THOUGHTS FOR MY BOOK:

SUN.

TIME	SCHEDULE

THOUGHTS FOR MY BOOK:

this week: _____

MON.	
TIME	SCHEDULE

TUE.	
TIME	SCHEDULE

WED.	
TIME	SCHEDULE

THOUGHTS FOR MY BOOK:

THOUGHTS FOR MY BOOK:

THOUGHTS FOR MY BOOK:

THU.

TIME	SCHEDULE

THOUGHTS FOR MY BOOK:

FRI.

TIME	SCHEDULE

THOUGHTS FOR MY BOOK:

SAT.

TIME	SCHEDULE

THOUGHTS FOR MY BOOK:

SUN.

TIME	SCHEDULE

THOUGHTS FOR MY BOOK:

this week: _____

MON.	
TIME	SCHEDULE

TUE.	
TIME	SCHEDULE

WED.	
TIME	SCHEDULE

THOUGHTS FOR MY BOOK:

THOUGHTS FOR MY BOOK:

THOUGHTS FOR MY BOOK:

THU.

TIME	SCHEDULE

THOUGHTS FOR MY BOOK:

FRI.

TIME	SCHEDULE

THOUGHTS FOR MY BOOK:

SAT.

TIME	SCHEDULE

THOUGHTS FOR MY BOOK:

SUN.

TIME	SCHEDULE

THOUGHTS FOR MY BOOK:

END OF MONTH *reflection*

this month:

MONTH:

YEAR:

SUNDAY	MONDAY	TUESDAY	WEDNESDAY	THURSDAY

FRIDAY	SATURDAY

notes

this week: _____

MON.	
TIME	SCHEDULE

TUE.	
TIME	SCHEDULE

WED.	
TIME	SCHEDULE

THOUGHTS FOR MY BOOK:

THOUGHTS FOR MY BOOK:

THOUGHTS FOR MY BOOK:

THU.

TIME	SCHEDULE

THOUGHTS FOR MY BOOK:

FRI.

TIME	SCHEDULE

THOUGHTS FOR MY BOOK:

SAT.

TIME	SCHEDULE

THOUGHTS FOR MY BOOK:

SUN.

TIME	SCHEDULE

THOUGHTS FOR MY BOOK:

this week: _____

MON.	
TIME	SCHEDULE

TUE.	
TIME	SCHEDULE

WED.	
TIME	SCHEDULE

THOUGHTS FOR MY BOOK:

THOUGHTS FOR MY BOOK:

THOUGHTS FOR MY BOOK:

THU.

TIME	SCHEDULE

THOUGHTS FOR MY BOOK:

FRI.

TIME	SCHEDULE

THOUGHTS FOR MY BOOK:

SAT.

TIME	SCHEDULE

THOUGHTS FOR MY BOOK:

SUN.

TIME	SCHEDULE

THOUGHTS FOR MY BOOK:

ND# this week: _____

MON.			TUE.			WED.	
TIME	SCHEDULE		TIME	SCHEDULE		TIME	SCHEDULE

THOUGHTS FOR MY BOOK:

_____
_____
_____
_____
_____
_____

THOUGHTS FOR MY BOOK:

_____
_____
_____
_____
_____
_____

THOUGHTS FOR MY BOOK:

_____
_____
_____
_____
_____
_____

THU.

TIME	SCHEDULE

THOUGHTS FOR MY BOOK:

FRI.

TIME	SCHEDULE

THOUGHTS FOR MY BOOK:

SAT.

TIME	SCHEDULE

THOUGHTS FOR MY BOOK:

SUN.

TIME	SCHEDULE

THOUGHTS FOR MY BOOK:

this week: _____

MON.	
TIME	SCHEDULE

TUE.	
TIME	SCHEDULE

WED.	
TIME	SCHEDULE

THOUGHTS FOR MY BOOK:

_____
_____
_____
_____
_____
_____
_____

THOUGHTS FOR MY BOOK:

_____
_____
_____
_____
_____
_____
_____

THOUGHTS FOR MY BOOK:

_____
_____
_____
_____
_____
_____
_____

THU.

TIME	SCHEDULE

THOUGHTS FOR MY BOOK:

FRI.

TIME	SCHEDULE

THOUGHTS FOR MY BOOK:

SAT.

TIME	SCHEDULE

THOUGHTS FOR MY BOOK:

SUN.

TIME	SCHEDULE

THOUGHTS FOR MY BOOK:

this week: _____

MON.	
TIME	SCHEDULE

TUE.	
TIME	SCHEDULE

WED.	
TIME	SCHEDULE

THOUGHTS FOR MY BOOK:

THOUGHTS FOR MY BOOK:

THOUGHTS FOR MY BOOK:

THU.

TIME	SCHEDULE

THOUGHTS FOR MY BOOK:

FRI.

TIME	SCHEDULE

THOUGHTS FOR MY BOOK:

SAT.

TIME	SCHEDULE

THOUGHTS FOR MY BOOK:

SUN.

TIME	SCHEDULE

THOUGHTS FOR MY BOOK:

END OF MONTH *reflection*

this month

MONTH: **YEAR:**

SUNDAY	MONDAY	TUESDAY	WEDNESDAY	THURSDAY

FRIDAY	SATURDAY

notes

this week: _____

MON.	
TIME	SCHEDULE

THOUGHTS FOR MY BOOK:

_____
_____
_____
_____
_____
_____
_____

TUE.	
TIME	SCHEDULE

THOUGHTS FOR MY BOOK:

_____
_____
_____
_____
_____
_____
_____

WED.	
TIME	SCHEDULE

THOUGHTS FOR MY BOOK:

_____
_____
_____
_____
_____
_____
_____

THU.

TIME	SCHEDULE

THOUGHTS FOR MY BOOK:

FRI.

TIME	SCHEDULE

THOUGHTS FOR MY BOOK:

SAT.

TIME	SCHEDULE

THOUGHTS FOR MY BOOK:

SUN.

TIME	SCHEDULE

THOUGHTS FOR MY BOOK:

this week: _____

MON.	
TIME	SCHEDULE

TUE.	
TIME	SCHEDULE

WED.	
TIME	SCHEDULE

THOUGHTS FOR MY BOOK:

THOUGHTS FOR MY BOOK:

THOUGHTS FOR MY BOOK:

THU.

TIME	SCHEDULE

THOUGHTS FOR MY BOOK:

FRI.

TIME	SCHEDULE

THOUGHTS FOR MY BOOK:

SAT.

TIME	SCHEDULE

THOUGHTS FOR MY BOOK:

SUN.

TIME	SCHEDULE

THOUGHTS FOR MY BOOK:

this week: _____

MON.	
TIME	SCHEDULE

TUE.	
TIME	SCHEDULE

WED.	
TIME	SCHEDULE

THOUGHTS FOR MY BOOK:

THOUGHTS FOR MY BOOK:

THOUGHTS FOR MY BOOK:

THU.

TIME	SCHEDULE

THOUGHTS FOR MY BOOK:

FRI.

TIME	SCHEDULE

THOUGHTS FOR MY BOOK:

SAT.

TIME	SCHEDULE

THOUGHTS FOR MY BOOK:

SUN.

TIME	SCHEDULE

THOUGHTS FOR MY BOOK:

this week: _____

MON.	
TIME	SCHEDULE

TUE.	
TIME	SCHEDULE

WED.	
TIME	SCHEDULE

THOUGHTS FOR MY BOOK:

THOUGHTS FOR MY BOOK:

THOUGHTS FOR MY BOOK:

THU.	
TIME	SCHEDULE

THOUGHTS FOR MY BOOK:

FRI.	
TIME	SCHEDULE

THOUGHTS FOR MY BOOK:

SAT.	
TIME	SCHEDULE

THOUGHTS FOR MY BOOK:

SUN.	
TIME	SCHEDULE

THOUGHTS FOR MY BOOK:

this week: _____

MON.	
TIME	SCHEDULE

TUE.	
TIME	SCHEDULE

WED.	
TIME	SCHEDULE

THOUGHTS FOR MY BOOK:

THOUGHTS FOR MY BOOK:

THOUGHTS FOR MY BOOK:

THU.

TIME	SCHEDULE

THOUGHTS FOR MY BOOK:

FRI.

TIME	SCHEDULE

THOUGHTS FOR MY BOOK:

SAT.

TIME	SCHEDULE

THOUGHTS FOR MY BOOK:

SUN.

TIME	SCHEDULE

THOUGHTS FOR MY BOOK:

END OF MONTH *reflection*

this month

MONTH: **YEAR:**

SUNDAY	MONDAY	TUESDAY	WEDNESDAY	THURSDAY

FRIDAY	SATURDAY

notes

this week: _____

MON.	
TIME	SCHEDULE

THOUGHTS FOR MY BOOK:

_____
_____
_____
_____
_____
_____
_____

TUE.	
TIME	SCHEDULE

THOUGHTS FOR MY BOOK:

_____
_____
_____
_____
_____
_____
_____

WED.	
TIME	SCHEDULE

THOUGHTS FOR MY BOOK:

_____
_____
_____
_____
_____
_____
_____

THU.

TIME	SCHEDULE

THOUGHTS FOR MY BOOK:

FRI.

TIME	SCHEDULE

THOUGHTS FOR MY BOOK:

SAT.

TIME	SCHEDULE

THOUGHTS FOR MY BOOK:

SUN.

TIME	SCHEDULE

THOUGHTS FOR MY BOOK:

this week: _____

MON.	
TIME	SCHEDULE

TUE.	
TIME	SCHEDULE

WED.	
TIME	SCHEDULE

THOUGHTS FOR MY BOOK:

THOUGHTS FOR MY BOOK:

THOUGHTS FOR MY BOOK:

THU.	
TIME	SCHEDULE

THOUGHTS FOR MY BOOK:

FRI.	
TIME	SCHEDULE

THOUGHTS FOR MY BOOK:

SAT.	
TIME	SCHEDULE

THOUGHTS FOR MY BOOK:

SUN.	
TIME	SCHEDULE

THOUGHTS FOR MY BOOK:

this week: _____

MON.	
TIME	SCHEDULE

THOUGHTS FOR MY BOOK:

_____
_____
_____
_____
_____
_____
_____

TUE.	
TIME	SCHEDULE

THOUGHTS FOR MY BOOK:

_____
_____
_____
_____
_____
_____
_____

WED.	
TIME	SCHEDULE

THOUGHTS FOR MY BOOK:

_____
_____
_____
_____
_____
_____
_____

THU.

TIME	SCHEDULE

THOUGHTS FOR MY BOOK:

FRI.

TIME	SCHEDULE

THOUGHTS FOR MY BOOK:

SAT.

TIME	SCHEDULE

THOUGHTS FOR MY BOOK:

SUN.

TIME	SCHEDULE

THOUGHTS FOR MY BOOK:

this week: _____

MON.	
TIME	SCHEDULE

THOUGHTS FOR MY BOOK:

_____
_____
_____
_____
_____
_____
_____

TUE.	
TIME	SCHEDULE

THOUGHTS FOR MY BOOK:

_____
_____
_____
_____
_____
_____
_____

WED.	
TIME	SCHEDULE

THOUGHTS FOR MY BOOK:

_____
_____
_____
_____
_____
_____
_____

THU.

TIME	SCHEDULE

THOUGHTS FOR MY BOOK:

FRI.

TIME	SCHEDULE

THOUGHTS FOR MY BOOK:

SAT.

TIME	SCHEDULE

THOUGHTS FOR MY BOOK:

SUN.

TIME	SCHEDULE

THOUGHTS FOR MY BOOK:

this week: _____

MON.	
TIME	SCHEDULE

TUE.	
TIME	SCHEDULE

WED.	
TIME	SCHEDULE

THOUGHTS FOR MY BOOK:

THOUGHTS FOR MY BOOK:

THOUGHTS FOR MY BOOK:

THU.

TIME	SCHEDULE

FRI.

TIME	SCHEDULE

SAT.

TIME	SCHEDULE

THOUGHTS FOR MY BOOK:

SUN.

TIME	SCHEDULE

THOUGHTS FOR MY BOOK:

THOUGHTS FOR MY BOOK:

THOUGHTS FOR MY BOOK:

END OF MONTH *reflection*

this month:

MONTH: **YEAR:**

SUNDAY	MONDAY	TUESDAY	WEDNESDAY	THURSDAY

FRIDAY	SATURDAY

notes

this week: _____

MON.	
TIME	SCHEDULE

THOUGHTS FOR MY BOOK:

_____
_____
_____
_____
_____
_____
_____
_____

TUE.	
TIME	SCHEDULE

THOUGHTS FOR MY BOOK:

_____
_____
_____
_____
_____
_____
_____
_____

WED.	
TIME	SCHEDULE

THOUGHTS FOR MY BOOK:

_____
_____
_____
_____
_____
_____
_____
_____

THU.

TIME	SCHEDULE

THOUGHTS FOR MY BOOK:

FRI.

TIME	SCHEDULE

THOUGHTS FOR MY BOOK:

SAT.

TIME	SCHEDULE

THOUGHTS FOR MY BOOK:

SUN.

TIME	SCHEDULE

THOUGHTS FOR MY BOOK:

this week: _____

MON.	
TIME	SCHEDULE

TUE.	
TIME	SCHEDULE

WED.	
TIME	SCHEDULE

THOUGHTS FOR MY BOOK:

THOUGHTS FOR MY BOOK:

THOUGHTS FOR MY BOOK:

THU.

TIME	SCHEDULE

THOUGHTS FOR MY BOOK:

FRI.

TIME	SCHEDULE

THOUGHTS FOR MY BOOK:

SAT.

TIME	SCHEDULE

THOUGHTS FOR MY BOOK:

SUN.

TIME	SCHEDULE

THOUGHTS FOR MY BOOK:

this week: _____

MON.	
TIME	SCHEDULE

TUE.	
TIME	SCHEDULE

WED.	
TIME	SCHEDULE

THOUGHTS FOR MY BOOK:

THOUGHTS FOR MY BOOK:

THOUGHTS FOR MY BOOK:

THU.

TIME	SCHEDULE

THOUGHTS FOR MY BOOK:

FRI.

TIME	SCHEDULE

THOUGHTS FOR MY BOOK:

SAT.

TIME	SCHEDULE

THOUGHTS FOR MY BOOK:

SUN.

TIME	SCHEDULE

THOUGHTS FOR MY BOOK:

this week: _____

MON.	
TIME	SCHEDULE

TUE.	
TIME	SCHEDULE

WED.	
TIME	SCHEDULE

THOUGHTS FOR MY BOOK:

THOUGHTS FOR MY BOOK:

THOUGHTS FOR MY BOOK:

THU.	
TIME	SCHEDULE

FRI.	
TIME	SCHEDULE

SAT.	
TIME	SCHEDULE

THOUGHTS FOR MY BOOK:

SUN.	
TIME	SCHEDULE

THOUGHTS FOR MY BOOK:

THOUGHTS FOR MY BOOK:

THOUGHTS FOR MY BOOK:

this week: _____

MON.	
TIME	SCHEDULE

TUE.	
TIME	SCHEDULE

WED.	
TIME	SCHEDULE

THOUGHTS FOR MY BOOK:

_____
_____
_____
_____
_____
_____
_____

THOUGHTS FOR MY BOOK:

_____
_____
_____
_____
_____
_____
_____

THOUGHTS FOR MY BOOK:

_____
_____
_____
_____
_____
_____
_____

THU.

TIME	SCHEDULE

THOUGHTS FOR MY BOOK:

FRI.

TIME	SCHEDULE

THOUGHTS FOR MY BOOK:

SAT.

TIME	SCHEDULE

THOUGHTS FOR MY BOOK:

SUN.

TIME	SCHEDULE

THOUGHTS FOR MY BOOK:

END OF MONTH *reflection*

this month:

MONTH: **YEAR:**

SUNDAY	MONDAY	TUESDAY	WEDNESDAY	THURSDAY

FRIDAY	SATURDAY

notes

this week: _____

MON.	
TIME	SCHEDULE

TUE.	
TIME	SCHEDULE

WED.	
TIME	SCHEDULE

THOUGHTS FOR MY BOOK:

THOUGHTS FOR MY BOOK:

THOUGHTS FOR MY BOOK:

THU.

TIME	SCHEDULE

THOUGHTS FOR MY BOOK:

FRI.

TIME	SCHEDULE

THOUGHTS FOR MY BOOK:

SAT.

TIME	SCHEDULE

THOUGHTS FOR MY BOOK:

SUN.

TIME	SCHEDULE

THOUGHTS FOR MY BOOK:

this week: _____

MON.	
TIME	SCHEDULE

TUE.	
TIME	SCHEDULE

WED.	
TIME	SCHEDULE

THOUGHTS FOR MY BOOK:

THOUGHTS FOR MY BOOK:

THOUGHTS FOR MY BOOK:

THU.

TIME	SCHEDULE

THOUGHTS FOR MY BOOK:

FRI.

TIME	SCHEDULE

THOUGHTS FOR MY BOOK:

SAT.

TIME	SCHEDULE

THOUGHTS FOR MY BOOK:

SUN.

TIME	SCHEDULE

THOUGHTS FOR MY BOOK:

this week: _____

MON.	
TIME	SCHEDULE

THOUGHTS FOR MY BOOK:

_____
_____
_____
_____
_____
_____
_____
_____

TUE.	
TIME	SCHEDULE

THOUGHTS FOR MY BOOK:

_____
_____
_____
_____
_____
_____
_____
_____

WED.	
TIME	SCHEDULE

THOUGHTS FOR MY BOOK:

_____
_____
_____
_____
_____
_____
_____
_____

THU.

TIME	SCHEDULE

FRI.

TIME	SCHEDULE

SAT.

TIME	SCHEDULE

THOUGHTS FOR MY BOOK:

SUN.

TIME	SCHEDULE

THOUGHTS FOR MY BOOK:

THOUGHTS FOR MY BOOK:

THOUGHTS FOR MY BOOK:

this week: _____

MON.	
TIME	SCHEDULE

THOUGHTS FOR MY BOOK:

_____
_____
_____
_____
_____
_____
_____

TUE.	
TIME	SCHEDULE

THOUGHTS FOR MY BOOK:

_____
_____
_____
_____
_____
_____
_____

WED.	
TIME	SCHEDULE

THOUGHTS FOR MY BOOK:

_____
_____
_____
_____
_____
_____
_____

THU.	
TIME	SCHEDULE

THOUGHTS FOR MY BOOK:

FRI.	
TIME	SCHEDULE

THOUGHTS FOR MY BOOK:

SAT.	
TIME	SCHEDULE

THOUGHTS FOR MY BOOK:

SUN.	
TIME	SCHEDULE

THOUGHTS FOR MY BOOK:

this week: _____

MON.	
TIME	SCHEDULE

THOUGHTS FOR MY BOOK:

_____
_____
_____
_____
_____
_____
_____
_____

TUE.	
TIME	SCHEDULE

THOUGHTS FOR MY BOOK:

_____
_____
_____
_____
_____
_____
_____
_____

WED.	
TIME	SCHEDULE

THOUGHTS FOR MY BOOK:

_____
_____
_____
_____
_____
_____
_____
_____

THU.

TIME	SCHEDULE

THOUGHTS FOR MY BOOK:

FRI.

TIME	SCHEDULE

THOUGHTS FOR MY BOOK:

SAT.

TIME	SCHEDULE

THOUGHTS FOR MY BOOK:

SUN.

TIME	SCHEDULE

THOUGHTS FOR MY BOOK:

END OF MONTH *reflection*

this month:

MONTH: **YEAR:**

SUNDAY	MONDAY	TUESDAY	WEDNESDAY	THURSDAY

FRIDAY	SATURDAY

notes

this week: _____

MON.	
TIME	SCHEDULE

TUE.	
TIME	SCHEDULE

WED.	
TIME	SCHEDULE

THOUGHTS FOR MY BOOK:

_____
_____
_____
_____
_____
_____
_____

THOUGHTS FOR MY BOOK:

_____
_____
_____
_____
_____
_____
_____

THOUGHTS FOR MY BOOK:

_____
_____
_____
_____
_____
_____
_____

THU.

TIME	SCHEDULE

THOUGHTS FOR MY BOOK:

FRI.

TIME	SCHEDULE

THOUGHTS FOR MY BOOK:

SAT.

TIME	SCHEDULE

THOUGHTS FOR MY BOOK:

SUN.

TIME	SCHEDULE

THOUGHTS FOR MY BOOK:

this week: _____

MON.	
TIME	SCHEDULE

TUE.	
TIME	SCHEDULE

WED.	
TIME	SCHEDULE

THOUGHTS FOR MY BOOK:

THOUGHTS FOR MY BOOK:

THOUGHTS FOR MY BOOK:

THU.

TIME	SCHEDULE

THOUGHTS FOR MY BOOK:

FRI.

TIME	SCHEDULE

THOUGHTS FOR MY BOOK:

SAT.

TIME	SCHEDULE

THOUGHTS FOR MY BOOK:

SUN.

TIME	SCHEDULE

THOUGHTS FOR MY BOOK:

this week: _____

MON.	
TIME	SCHEDULE

THOUGHTS FOR MY BOOK:

_____
_____
_____
_____
_____
_____
_____

TUE.	
TIME	SCHEDULE

THOUGHTS FOR MY BOOK:

_____
_____
_____
_____
_____
_____
_____

WED.	
TIME	SCHEDULE

THOUGHTS FOR MY BOOK:

_____
_____
_____
_____
_____
_____
_____

THU.

TIME	SCHEDULE

THOUGHTS FOR MY BOOK:

FRI.

TIME	SCHEDULE

THOUGHTS FOR MY BOOK:

SAT.

TIME	SCHEDULE

THOUGHTS FOR MY BOOK:

SUN.

TIME	SCHEDULE

THOUGHTS FOR MY BOOK:

this week: _____

MON.	
TIME	SCHEDULE

THOUGHTS FOR MY BOOK:

_____
_____
_____
_____
_____
_____
_____

TUE.	
TIME	SCHEDULE

THOUGHTS FOR MY BOOK:

_____
_____
_____
_____
_____
_____
_____

WED.	
TIME	SCHEDULE

THOUGHTS FOR MY BOOK:

_____
_____
_____
_____
_____
_____
_____

THU.

TIME	SCHEDULE

THOUGHTS FOR MY BOOK:

FRI.

TIME	SCHEDULE

THOUGHTS FOR MY BOOK:

SAT.

TIME	SCHEDULE

THOUGHTS FOR MY BOOK:

SUN.

TIME	SCHEDULE

THOUGHTS FOR MY BOOK:

this week: _____

MON.	
TIME	SCHEDULE

TUE.	
TIME	SCHEDULE

WED.	
TIME	SCHEDULE

THOUGHTS FOR MY BOOK:

THOUGHTS FOR MY BOOK:

THOUGHTS FOR MY BOOK:

THU.

TIME	SCHEDULE

THOUGHTS FOR MY BOOK:

FRI.

TIME	SCHEDULE

THOUGHTS FOR MY BOOK:

SAT.

TIME	SCHEDULE

THOUGHTS FOR MY BOOK:

SUN.

TIME	SCHEDULE

THOUGHTS FOR MY BOOK:

END OF MONTH *reflection*

this month:

MONTH: **YEAR:**

SUNDAY	MONDAY	TUESDAY	WEDNESDAY	THURSDAY

FRIDAY	SATURDAY

notes

this week: _____

MON.			TUE.			WED.	
TIME	SCHEDULE		TIME	SCHEDULE		TIME	SCHEDULE

THOUGHTS FOR MY BOOK:

THOUGHTS FOR MY BOOK:

THOUGHTS FOR MY BOOK:

THU.

TIME	SCHEDULE

THOUGHTS FOR MY BOOK:

FRI.

TIME	SCHEDULE

THOUGHTS FOR MY BOOK:

SAT.

TIME	SCHEDULE

THOUGHTS FOR MY BOOK:

SUN.

TIME	SCHEDULE

THOUGHTS FOR MY BOOK:

this week: _____

MON.	
TIME	SCHEDULE

TUE.	
TIME	SCHEDULE

WED.	
TIME	SCHEDULE

THOUGHTS FOR MY BOOK:

THOUGHTS FOR MY BOOK:

THOUGHTS FOR MY BOOK:

THU.	
TIME	SCHEDULE

THOUGHTS FOR MY BOOK:

FRI.	
TIME	SCHEDULE

THOUGHTS FOR MY BOOK:

SAT.	
TIME	SCHEDULE

THOUGHTS FOR MY BOOK:

SUN.	
TIME	SCHEDULE

THOUGHTS FOR MY BOOK:

this week: _____

MON.	
TIME	SCHEDULE

THOUGHTS FOR MY BOOK:

_____
_____
_____
_____
_____
_____
_____
_____

TUE.	
TIME	SCHEDULE

THOUGHTS FOR MY BOOK:

_____
_____
_____
_____
_____
_____
_____
_____

WED.	
TIME	SCHEDULE

THOUGHTS FOR MY BOOK:

_____
_____
_____
_____
_____
_____
_____
_____

THU.

TIME	SCHEDULE

FRI.

TIME	SCHEDULE

SAT.

TIME	SCHEDULE

THOUGHTS FOR MY BOOK:

SUN.

TIME	SCHEDULE

THOUGHTS FOR MY BOOK:

THOUGHTS FOR MY BOOK:

THOUGHTS FOR MY BOOK:

this week: _____

MON.	
TIME	SCHEDULE

TUE.	
TIME	SCHEDULE

WED.	
TIME	SCHEDULE

THOUGHTS FOR MY BOOK:

THOUGHTS FOR MY BOOK:

THOUGHTS FOR MY BOOK:

THU.

TIME	SCHEDULE

THOUGHTS FOR MY BOOK:

FRI.

TIME	SCHEDULE

THOUGHTS FOR MY BOOK:

SAT.

TIME	SCHEDULE

THOUGHTS FOR MY BOOK:

SUN.

TIME	SCHEDULE

THOUGHTS FOR MY BOOK:

this week: _____

MON.	
TIME	SCHEDULE

TUE.	
TIME	SCHEDULE

WED.	
TIME	SCHEDULE

THOUGHTS FOR MY BOOK:

THOUGHTS FOR MY BOOK:

THOUGHTS FOR MY BOOK:

THU.

TIME	SCHEDULE

THOUGHTS FOR MY BOOK:

FRI.

TIME	SCHEDULE

THOUGHTS FOR MY BOOK:

SAT.

TIME	SCHEDULE

THOUGHTS FOR MY BOOK:

SUN.

TIME	SCHEDULE

THOUGHTS FOR MY BOOK:

END OF MONTH *reflection*

this month:

MONTH: **YEAR:**

SUNDAY	MONDAY	TUESDAY	WEDNESDAY	THURSDAY

FRIDAY	SATURDAY

notes

this week: _____

MON.	
TIME	SCHEDULE

TUE.	
TIME	SCHEDULE

WED.	
TIME	SCHEDULE

THOUGHTS FOR MY BOOK:

THOUGHTS FOR MY BOOK:

THOUGHTS FOR MY BOOK:

THU.

TIME	SCHEDULE

THOUGHTS FOR MY BOOK:

FRI.

TIME	SCHEDULE

THOUGHTS FOR MY BOOK:

SAT.

TIME	SCHEDULE

THOUGHTS FOR MY BOOK:

SUN.

TIME	SCHEDULE

THOUGHTS FOR MY BOOK:

this week: _____

MON.			TUE.			WED.	
TIME	SCHEDULE		TIME	SCHEDULE		TIME	SCHEDULE

THOUGHTS FOR MY BOOK:

THOUGHTS FOR MY BOOK:

THOUGHTS FOR MY BOOK:

THU.

TIME	SCHEDULE

THOUGHTS FOR MY BOOK:

FRI.

TIME	SCHEDULE

THOUGHTS FOR MY BOOK:

SAT.

TIME	SCHEDULE

THOUGHTS FOR MY BOOK:

SUN.

TIME	SCHEDULE

THOUGHTS FOR MY BOOK:

this week: _____

MON.	
TIME	SCHEDULE

TUE.	
TIME	SCHEDULE

WED.	
TIME	SCHEDULE

THOUGHTS FOR MY BOOK:

THOUGHTS FOR MY BOOK:

THOUGHTS FOR MY BOOK:

THU.

TIME	SCHEDULE

THOUGHTS FOR MY BOOK:

FRI.

TIME	SCHEDULE

THOUGHTS FOR MY BOOK:

SAT.

TIME	SCHEDULE

THOUGHTS FOR MY BOOK:

SUN.

TIME	SCHEDULE

THOUGHTS FOR MY BOOK:

this week: _____

MON.	
TIME	SCHEDULE

TUE.	
TIME	SCHEDULE

WED.	
TIME	SCHEDULE

THOUGHTS FOR MY BOOK:

THOUGHTS FOR MY BOOK:

THOUGHTS FOR MY BOOK:

THU.

TIME	SCHEDULE

THOUGHTS FOR MY BOOK:

FRI.

TIME	SCHEDULE

THOUGHTS FOR MY BOOK:

SAT.

TIME	SCHEDULE

THOUGHTS FOR MY BOOK:

SUN.

TIME	SCHEDULE

THOUGHTS FOR MY BOOK:

this week: _____

MON.	
TIME	SCHEDULE

TUE.	
TIME	SCHEDULE

WED.	
TIME	SCHEDULE

THOUGHTS FOR MY BOOK:

THOUGHTS FOR MY BOOK:

THOUGHTS FOR MY BOOK:

THU.

TIME	SCHEDULE

THOUGHTS FOR MY BOOK:

FRI.

TIME	SCHEDULE

THOUGHTS FOR MY BOOK:

SAT.

TIME	SCHEDULE

THOUGHTS FOR MY BOOK:

SUN.

TIME	SCHEDULE

THOUGHTS FOR MY BOOK:

END OF MONTH *reflection*

this month:

MONTH:

YEAR:

SUNDAY	MONDAY	TUESDAY	WEDNESDAY	THURSDAY

FRIDAY	SATURDAY

notes

this week: _____

MON.	
TIME	SCHEDULE |––

TUE.	
TIME	SCHEDULE

WED.	
TIME	SCHEDULE

THOUGHTS FOR MY BOOK:

THOUGHTS FOR MY BOOK:

THOUGHTS FOR MY BOOK:

THU.

TIME	SCHEDULE

THOUGHTS FOR MY BOOK:

FRI.

TIME	SCHEDULE

THOUGHTS FOR MY BOOK:

SAT.

TIME	SCHEDULE

THOUGHTS FOR MY BOOK:

SUN.

TIME	SCHEDULE

THOUGHTS FOR MY BOOK:

this week: _____

MON.	
TIME	SCHEDULE

TUE.	
TIME	SCHEDULE

WED.	
TIME	SCHEDULE

THOUGHTS FOR MY BOOK:

THOUGHTS FOR MY BOOK:

THOUGHTS FOR MY BOOK:

THU.

TIME	SCHEDULE

THOUGHTS FOR MY BOOK:

FRI.

TIME	SCHEDULE

THOUGHTS FOR MY BOOK:

SAT.

TIME	SCHEDULE

THOUGHTS FOR MY BOOK:

SUN.

TIME	SCHEDULE

THOUGHTS FOR MY BOOK:

this week: _____

MON.			TUE.			WED.	
TIME	SCHEDULE		TIME	SCHEDULE		TIME	SCHEDULE

THOUGHTS FOR MY BOOK:

THOUGHTS FOR MY BOOK:

THOUGHTS FOR MY BOOK:

THU.

TIME	SCHEDULE

THOUGHTS FOR MY BOOK:

FRI.

TIME	SCHEDULE

THOUGHTS FOR MY BOOK:

SAT.

TIME	SCHEDULE

THOUGHTS FOR MY BOOK:

SUN.

TIME	SCHEDULE

THOUGHTS FOR MY BOOK:

this week: _____

MON.	
TIME	SCHEDULE

THOUGHTS FOR MY BOOK:

_____
_____
_____
_____
_____
_____
_____

TUE.	
TIME	SCHEDULE

THOUGHTS FOR MY BOOK:

_____
_____
_____
_____
_____
_____
_____

WED.	
TIME	SCHEDULE

THOUGHTS FOR MY BOOK:

_____
_____
_____
_____
_____
_____
_____

THU.

TIME	SCHEDULE

THOUGHTS FOR MY BOOK:

FRI.

TIME	SCHEDULE

THOUGHTS FOR MY BOOK:

SAT.

TIME	SCHEDULE

THOUGHTS FOR MY BOOK:

SUN.

TIME	SCHEDULE

THOUGHTS FOR MY BOOK:

this week: _____

MON.	
TIME	SCHEDULE

TUE.	
TIME	SCHEDULE

WED.	
TIME	SCHEDULE

THOUGHTS FOR MY BOOK:

THOUGHTS FOR MY BOOK:

THOUGHTS FOR MY BOOK:

THU.

TIME	SCHEDULE

THOUGHTS FOR MY BOOK:

FRI.

TIME	SCHEDULE

THOUGHTS FOR MY BOOK:

SAT.

TIME	SCHEDULE

THOUGHTS FOR MY BOOK:

SUN.

TIME	SCHEDULE

THOUGHTS FOR MY BOOK:

END OF MONTH *reflection*

this month:

MONTH:

YEAR:

SUNDAY	MONDAY	TUESDAY	WEDNESDAY	THURSDAY

FRIDAY	SATURDAY

notes

this week: _____

MON.	
TIME	SCHEDULE

THOUGHTS FOR MY BOOK:

_____
_____
_____
_____
_____
_____
_____

TUE.	
TIME	SCHEDULE

THOUGHTS FOR MY BOOK:

_____
_____
_____
_____
_____
_____
_____

WED.	
TIME	SCHEDULE

THOUGHTS FOR MY BOOK:

_____
_____
_____
_____
_____
_____
_____

THU.

TIME	SCHEDULE

THOUGHTS FOR MY BOOK:

FRI.

TIME	SCHEDULE

THOUGHTS FOR MY BOOK:

SAT.

TIME	SCHEDULE

THOUGHTS FOR MY BOOK:

SUN.

TIME	SCHEDULE

THOUGHTS FOR MY BOOK:

this week: _____

MON.			TUE.			WED.	
TIME	SCHEDULE		TIME	SCHEDULE		TIME	SCHEDULE

THOUGHTS FOR MY BOOK:

THOUGHTS FOR MY BOOK:

THOUGHTS FOR MY BOOK:

THU.

TIME	SCHEDULE

FRI.

TIME	SCHEDULE

SAT.

TIME	SCHEDULE

THOUGHTS FOR MY BOOK:

SUN.

TIME	SCHEDULE

THOUGHTS FOR MY BOOK:

THOUGHTS FOR MY BOOK:

THOUGHTS FOR MY BOOK:

this week: _____

MON.	
TIME	SCHEDULE

THOUGHTS FOR MY BOOK:

_____
_____
_____
_____
_____
_____
_____

TUE.	
TIME	SCHEDULE

THOUGHTS FOR MY BOOK:

_____
_____
_____
_____
_____
_____
_____

WED.	
TIME	SCHEDULE

THOUGHTS FOR MY BOOK:

_____
_____
_____
_____
_____
_____
_____

THU.

TIME	SCHEDULE

THOUGHTS FOR MY BOOK:

FRI.

TIME	SCHEDULE

THOUGHTS FOR MY BOOK:

SAT.

TIME	SCHEDULE

THOUGHTS FOR MY BOOK:

SUN.

TIME	SCHEDULE

THOUGHTS FOR MY BOOK:

this week: _____

MON.	
TIME	SCHEDULE

TUE.	
TIME	SCHEDULE

WED.	
TIME	SCHEDULE

THOUGHTS FOR MY BOOK:

THOUGHTS FOR MY BOOK:

THOUGHTS FOR MY BOOK:

THU.

TIME	SCHEDULE

THOUGHTS FOR MY BOOK:

FRI.

TIME	SCHEDULE

THOUGHTS FOR MY BOOK:

SAT.

TIME	SCHEDULE

THOUGHTS FOR MY BOOK:

SUN.

TIME	SCHEDULE

THOUGHTS FOR MY BOOK:

this week: _____

MON.	
TIME	SCHEDULE

TUE.	
TIME	SCHEDULE

WED.	
TIME	SCHEDULE

THOUGHTS FOR MY BOOK:

THOUGHTS FOR MY BOOK:

THOUGHTS FOR MY BOOK:

THU.

TIME	SCHEDULE

THOUGHTS FOR MY BOOK:

FRI.

TIME	SCHEDULE

THOUGHTS FOR MY BOOK:

SAT.

TIME	SCHEDULE

THOUGHTS FOR MY BOOK:

SUN.

TIME	SCHEDULE

THOUGHTS FOR MY BOOK:

END OF MONTH *reflection*

GO LAUNCH *your* STORYBOOK!!

notes